I0142237

Hi kids... Let's have some fun learning your numbers.

I will help you, so let's get started and have some FUN !

1 ONE

Buddy has a favorite hat to help keep the sun out of his eyes, can you count how many hats there are ?

2 TWO

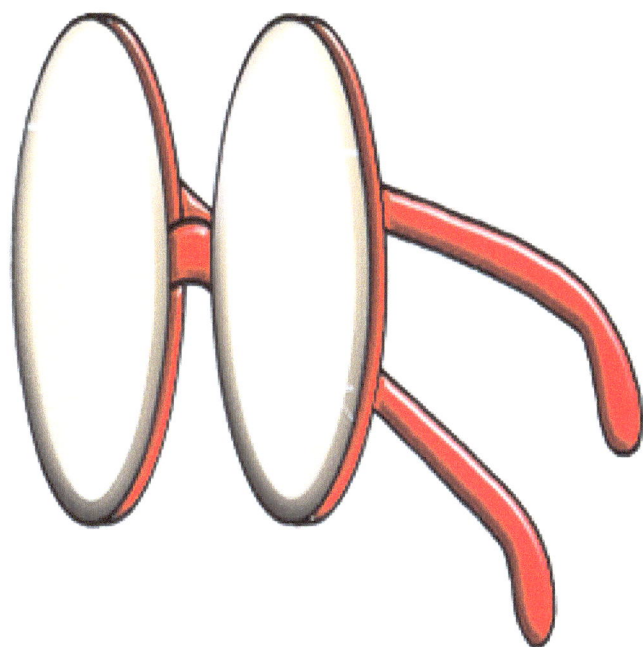

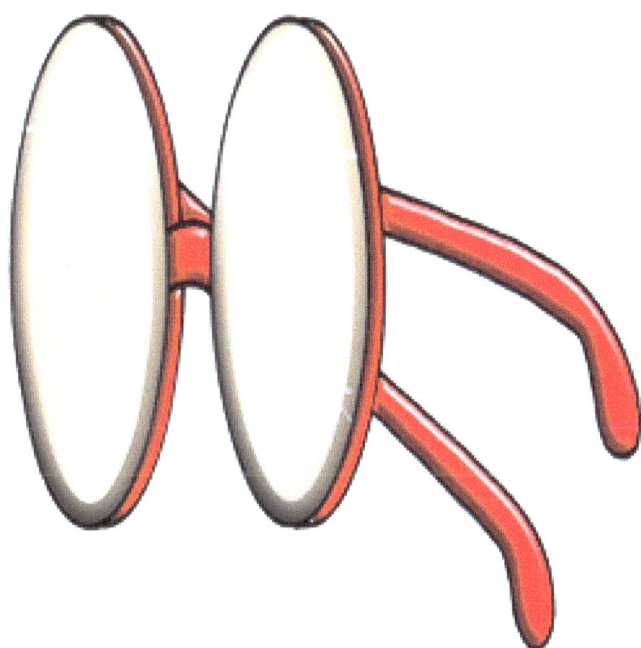

Buddy wears special glasses to help him see, how many glasses do you see ?

BW

3 THREE

Buddy loves his red shoes. They help him walk because Buddy can't fly very well. How many shoes can you count?

4 FOUR

Buddy loves to make honey. How many jars of honey has buddy made?

5 FIVE

Buddy lives in a Bee Hive. How many Bee Hives can you count?

Buddy loves flowers. Buddy gets his food from flowers.How many Yellow flowers can you count ?

7 SEVEN

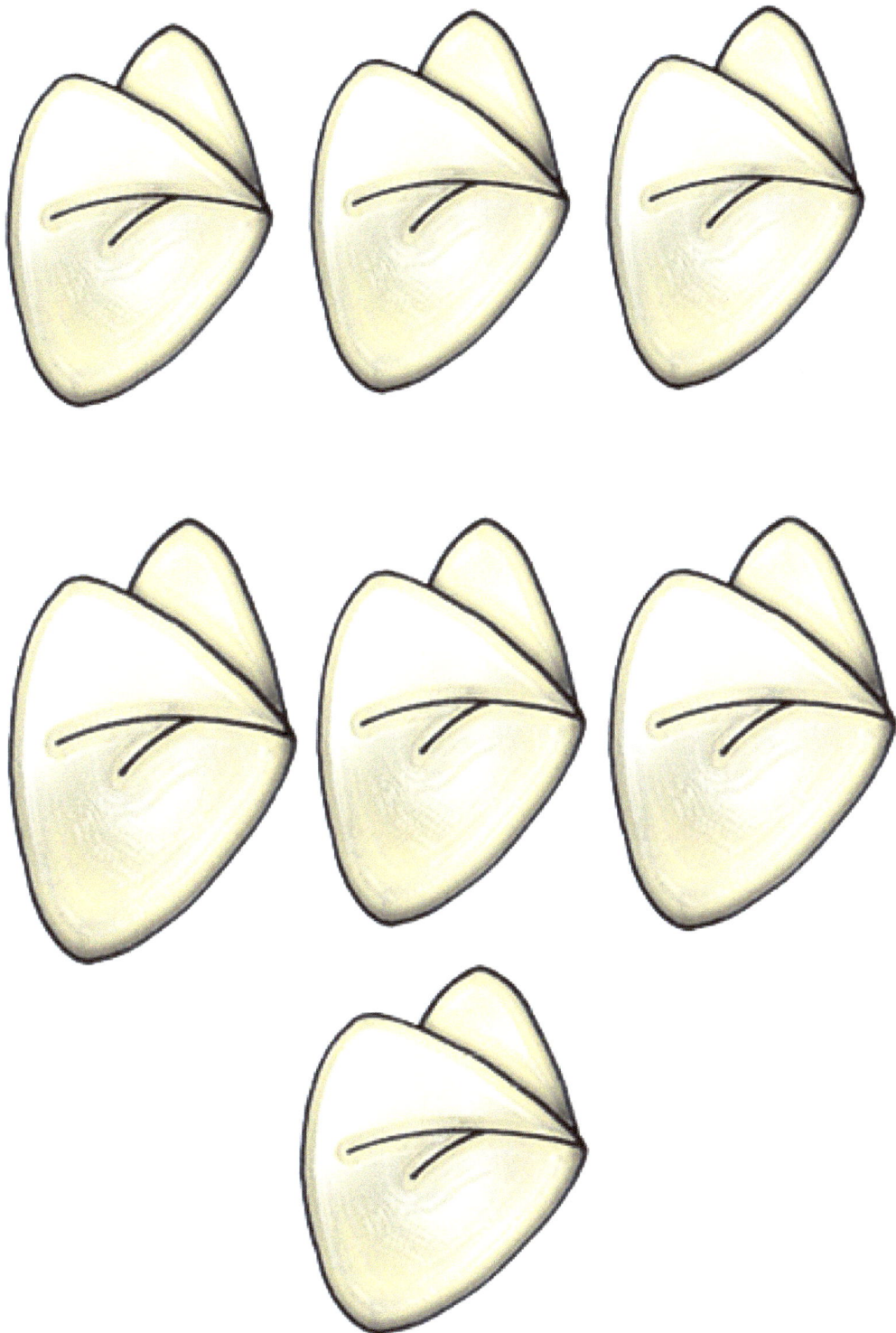

Buddy is not like most Bumble Bees, he was born with smaller wings and can't fly. How many wings can you count ?

8 EIGHT

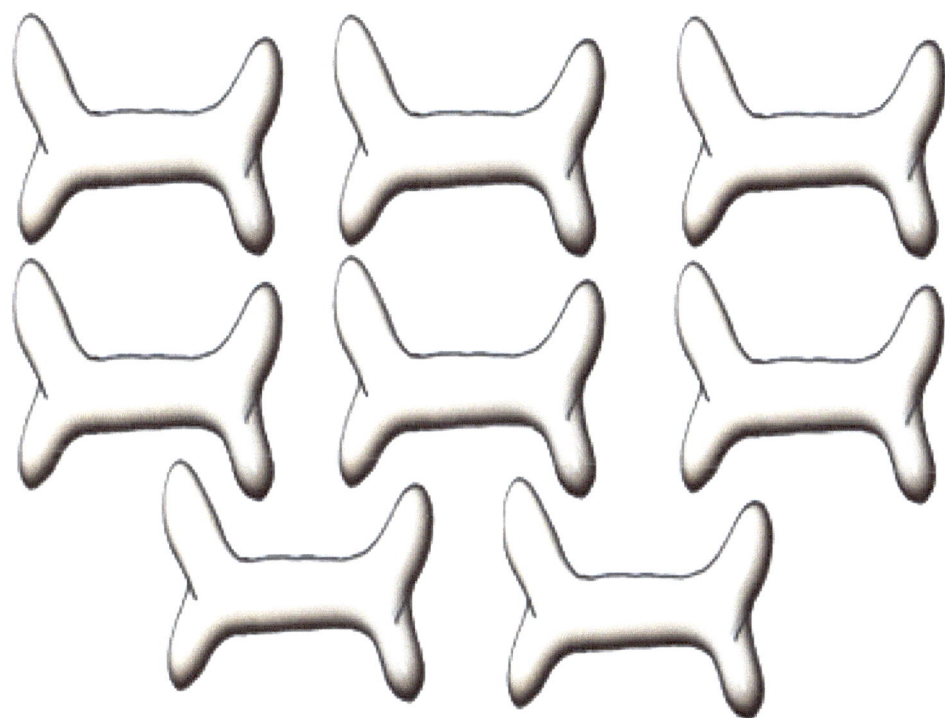

Schnoodle is Buddys dog and likes to bury bones. How many bones does Schnoodle have to bury today ?

9 NINE

A Close friend to Buddy is Suzzy Bee. Suzzy loves ribbons and bows. She loves to collect bows for all her friends. Can you count how many she has ?

Friends are very important to have and Buddy has a lot of them. Can you count all his friends?

Thank you for counting with me. I hope you had fun and
my book helped you. Remember to always ask your teacher
or parents for help ! Math is very important and we're here
to help you.

Have a Hapbee Day,

Buddy Bee

www.ingramcontent.com/pod-product-compliance
Lightning Source LLC
LaVergne TN
LVHW010024070426

835508LV00001B/51